Rights in the Home

What do we mean by human rights?

Emma Haughton & Penny Clarke

SEA-TO-SEA

Mankato Collingwood London

This edition first published in 2006 by
Sea-to-Sea Publications
1980 Lookout Drive
North Mankato
Minnesota 56003

Printed in China

Library of Congress Cataloging-in-Publication Data

Haughton, Emma.
  Rights in the home / by Emma Haughton & Penny Clarke.
    p. cm. — (What do we mean by human rights?)
  Originally published: New York: Franklin Watts, 1997.
  Includes index.
  ISBN 1-932889-65-5
  1. Human rights—Juvenile literature. 2. Homelessness—Juvenile literature. 3.
  Domestic relations—Juvenile literature. 4. Children's rights—Juvenile literature.
    I. Clarke, Penny. II. Title. III. Series.

JC571.H355 2005
323—dc22

                                              2004063636

9 8 7 6 5 4 3 2

Published by arrangement with the Watts Publishing Group Ltd, London

Acknowledgments::

Extended family life, *The Independent*, May 6, 1996; An arrangement for life, *The Independent*, October 27, 1995; Mali, *Telegraph Magazine*, October 26, 1996; Eglantyne Jebb, Save the Children publicity material; Emma Humphreys, *The Independent*, July 8 1995; Care for the elderly, Action on Elder Abuse; Mexico, *The Times*, September 1996.

"Save the Children" logo (p.27) is registered in the UK and produced with kind permission from Save the Children.

Picture credits:

Cover and title page: Magnum Photos (Dennis Stock)

Eye Ubiquitous 13, 23 B, 36 (James Davis Travel Photography); Robert Harding Picture Library 12B, 25B, 29B; Robert Harding Syndication 25T (Caroline Penn/Marie Claire); David Hoffman 34, 35L; Hulton Getty Collection 7B, 9B, 28T; Magnum Photos 5 (Dennis Stock), 7T (Chris Steele-Perkins), 11T (Ernst Haas), 12T (Eugene Richards), 14T (Raghu Rai), 16B (H. Gruyaert), 28B (Burt Glenn), 31T (Steve McCurry), 31B (Eli Reed), 37 (Paul Fusco), 41R (Luc Delahaye);

Panos Pictures 6T (Penny Tweedie), 6BL (Philip Wolmuth), 9T (Penny Tweedie), 11B (Jeremy Hartley), 22B (Wang Gangfeng), 23C (J.C. Callow), 24B (Paul Harrison), 33T, 35R, 38B & 39B (Philip Wolmuth); Rex Features 6BR, 8T, 14B, 15T& B, 17T & B, 18, 19T & B, 20T & B, 21T & B, 22T, 23T, 24T, 26, 29T, 30T & B, 32, 33B, 36-37, 38T, 43R; Save the Children Fund 27T & B; Topham Picturepoint 10, 16T, 39T (Press Association) 40, 41L, 42L & R, 43L; John Walmsley 8B, 16T.

CONTENTS

Home is something most of us take for granted. It is where we live, eat, relax, and sleep. But a home is much more than four walls and a roof to keep the weather out. Home is somewhere you should feel you belong, somewhere you should feel safe. Feelings of security come from your family: people to whom you can turn for support and comfort when you need it, just as you would help them if they needed it. Your family forms another part of your home.

A woman in Bangladesh surveys the flooded ruins of her home. She and her child are safe, but how will she be able to care for him? Losing your home, for whatever reason, can have a devastating effect.

The ideal and the reality

That is the ideal, but sadly this is not true for many people throughout the world. A home, whether in its obvious physical form, a house or dwelling, or as that vital feeling of being part of a family, of belonging, can easily be destroyed. Sometimes the destruction is caused by outside forces, such as wars and natural disasters, that we are powerless to control. All too often, vivid pictures on television screens show people who have seen their homes destroyed and their families scattered.

Homes come in many shapes and sizes, but what they look like is not the most important thing about them. The feeling of security, of belonging, that a good home gives every member of the family is what really matters.

But a home can be destroyed just as effectively by events that never reach the media. Being laid off at work or losing their job can force people from their homes because they can no longer pay the rent or the mortgage. Some women leave their homes because their partners are violent. Young people may leave to escape serious arguments or abuse. In each of these situations, homes (in both senses of the word) are destroyed just as effectively as if they had been swept away in a flood.

While efforts to protect people throughout the world continue, whole communities, such as these Rwandan refugees, still find themselves fleeing their homes in search of safety.

(Below) A Jewish prisoner gasps for breath as oxygen is denied him in a Nazi concentration camp; Nazis claimed these cruel acts were for "scientific research."

Losing a home

Losing a home is a disaster for the family concerned, but, for society as a whole, the breakdown of the family unit can have far wider effects. Too often, people without a settled base from which to draw affection and support find it difficult to give others the support that they themselves lack. This becomes a vicious circle that is hard to break.

What are human rights?

It is probably true to say that no one questions the importance of a home to the well-being of each one of us. Therefore, it can be argued that each one of us has the right to a home. So, if we each have such a right, it must be a universal human right. But what is a human right?

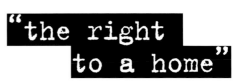
"the right to a home"

Human rights are basic standards that all people should be able to expect in their lives. During the Second World War, different groups within society were persecuted under the Nazi government in Germany. At the end of the war, there was a universal upsurge of feeling that the atrocities committed should not be allowed to happen again. As a result, in 1945 more than 50 countries got together to form the United Nations (UN). On December 10, 1948 the UN agreed the Universal Declaration of Human Rights (UDHR) as "a common standard of achievement for all peoples and all nations."

The UN in session, New York. It has done an enormous amount to draw attention to human rights—and to their abuse.

The Universal Declaration of Human Rights

The Declaration is divided into 30 Articles. It includes most of the different issues that we call human rights. It covers issues of equality, such as race and sex; economic issues, including work, leisure, property, food, housing, and health; issues of justice, such as the right to a proper trial; and issues of belief, including religion, politics, and freedom to think and speak. It also covers personal matters, such as the rights concerning the family and marriage.

Every one of these subjects is a human right. The intention of the Declaration is to ensure that people everywhere have what they need to live their lives in peace and dignity, free from fear and overwhelming hardship. That is why it is called The "Universal" Declaration of Human Rights.

a universal declaration"

Many people regard the Declaration as one of the greatest achievements of the twentieth century. Although the Declaration is not law, it sets clear standards for all countries and governments to aim for. It also has a strong message for each one of us. Human rights are not just about our rights, they are about the rights of others, too. It is our responsibility to make sure other people are treated fairly.

The UDHR recognizes the significance of day-to-day issues, such as the availability of good health care to ensure quality of life.

While many of the articles are relevant, these are the main clauses of the Universal Declaration of Human Rights that are concerned with rights in the home:

Article 12
No one shall be subjected to arbitrary interference with his privacy, family, home, or correspondence, nor to attacks upon his honor and reputation. Everyone has the right to the protection of the law against such interference or attacks.

Article 16
1. Men and women of full age, without any limitations due to race, nationality, or religion, have the right to marry and to found a family. They are entitled to equal rights as to marriage, during marriage, and at its dissolution.
2. Marriage shall be entered into only with the free and full consent of the intending spouses.
3. The family is the natural and fundamental group unit of society and is entitled to protection by society and the State.

Article 25
1. Everyone has the right to a standard of living adequate for the health and well-being of himself and of his family, including food, clothing, housing and medical care, and necessary social services, and the right to security in the event of unemployment, sickness, disability, widowhood, old age, or other lack of livelihood in circumstances beyond his control.

2. Motherhood and childhood are entitled to special care and assistance. All children, whether born in or out of wedlock, shall enjoy the same social protection.

The home and human rights

Eleanor Roosevelt, the wife of President Franklin D. Roosevelt, highlighted the significance of human rights and our responsibility toward upholding them when she said: "Where, after all, do human rights begin? In small places, close to home—so close and so small that they cannot be seen on any maps of the world." She was a member of the committee that first drew up the UDHR. And she recognized that rights need protecting in the "small places" every bit as much as they do on the world stage.

The following chapters explore just how the Declaration applies to rights in the home—in the very widest sense of that word—and the responsibilities that these rights bring.

Eleanor Roosevelt (1884–1962) worked to ensure a decent standard of living for everyone.

HOME AND FAMILY

On a smallholding in France, Elizabeth Vincent and her husband Alain have welcomed their adult daughters, Valerie and Isabelle, back home—with their husbands and children.

Valerie, her husband, Philippe, and their two children have moved to a house on the edge of the smallholding. Five hundred yards down the road, Isabelle lives with her husband Eric and their children.

Child's play? Or perhaps a better way to bring up a family, as the Vincents of Brittany believe.

Valerie and Isabelle took the decision with their husbands to move back to the family farm when their children were born because they felt the benefit of living within an extended family would be tremendous—for all concerned.

"nuclear families"

While Valerie and Philippe and Isabelle and Eric go out to work, Elizabeth and Alain run their smallholding with the help of their grandchildren. When not at school, the children help feed the animals or ride around on their bikes in the safety of the yard. A list nailed to the back of the shed door reminds Elizabeth when to pick up the children from school or daycare.

Elizabeth has always encouraged her daughters to pursue their own careers. Isabelle believes she is in a very privileged position. "It's a wonderful arrangement because as well as having the love and support of their own nuclear families, our children have the continuous care of their grandparents who will always love them and be an important part of their lives."

Elizabeth does take on much of the responsibility of childcare during the week—an issue that sometimes worries her daughters. "But we hope that in the future we will be here for our parents when they need us: not because we feel obliged to but because we want to. That is, after all, what the extended family is all about."

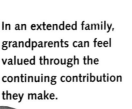

In an extended family, grandparents can feel valued through the continuing contribution they make.

The family unit

Extended families, such as the Vincent family's arrangement, were common in the developed world until quite recently. Children were looked after by aunts, cousins, and grandparents and not just by their parents. This eased the strains on parents as the workload and responsibilities were shared. It also gave grandparents a useful and respected place in the family, with their knowledge and experience being valued. Indeed, this family setup is still very important in some cultures. In many Asian and African families this structure still operates—with parents often relying on the wider support of their relatives to contribute to the running of the household.

Article 16 (3) of the UDHR acknowledges that "the family is the natural and fundamental group unit of society and is entitled to protection by society and the State." But what is a family? As the Vincents show, it is not unchanging and can take many different forms.

Three generations of an extended family in Senegal, West Africa. Here, as in many other cultures, large extended families are the rule, unlike many western countries where the small, nuclear family, is now common.

(Right) The family has traditionally played a part in disciplining and shaping its members. With the breakdown of the traditional family unit in many developed countries, some governments are concerned that this important role has become weakened.

(Below) Stresses of modern life add to the demands and changes within a family.

Changing patterns

In the developed world changing work patterns, more wealth, better public transportation, and particularly in the last 30 years, the dramatic growth in the ownership of cars and telephones, have made it easier for families to live apart and still maintain contact.

However, as such social changes have become part of society, the family unit has also changed. Today's small "nuclear" family of two parents and one or two children, usual in the developed world, is relatively new. Now single-parent families are common—where adults have separated or divorced or sometimes opted to start a family without necessarily being in an established partnership. As divorces have increased, the number of "second" and even "third" families and step-families has grown.

Protecting the family unit

While the make-up of a family has taken on many different shapes, the function of most families remains the same. The family unit, in whatever form, is considered central to our individual development. It is the place where we learn how to behave and so how to relate to the world around us. That is why the UDHR acknowledges that it is crucial to protect this "fundamental group unit of society." However, as it can be difficult to define a family, it can also be difficult for governments to ensure that all rights within a family are upheld. Similarly, it can be difficult to ensure that people's rights within a partnership, the basis of family life, are recognized.

MARRIAGE AND THE FAMILY

Date:
2002
Place:
Scotland
Issue:
Arranged
marriage

Aneeka Sohrab, a 16-year-old schoolgirl in Glasgow, was told she would be married a week before the ceremony. Against her will, her parents had arranged for her to wed Raja Sulman Khan, 19, from Pakistan, so he could remain in the UK. Aneeka became hysterical and wept, but her mother theatened to put her out of the house for bringing shame on the family. Worse, her mother vowed to commit suicide. So Aneeka and Raja married at a Glasgow mosque on December 13, 1998.

However, the girl remained very upset, and the couple separated after the marriage was only four months old. Aneeka's family went to court and the judge annulled the marriage on April 23, 2002. He said the two young people were "under an intolerable pressure at an age when neither was able to take an informed decision about their future and neither was in a position to resist the will of their parents."

Aneeka is now employed by ScottishPower and studies at college. Estimates say up to 1,000 British Asian women are forced to marry each year, and relatives often become violent if they rebel. About 20 murders in the past decade involved the breakdowns of arranged marriages. As the judge in Aneeka's case added: "It may be that in the multicultural society in which we now live, such situations will continue to arise where ancient Eastern established cultural and religious ethics clash with the spirit of 21st-century children of a new generation."

"Her mother threatened to put her out of the house"

Being part of two cultures can be very difficult. While parents may wish to keep their own culture, their children may be attracted by the culture in which they have grown up.

An important union

Traditionally, throughout different countries and cultures, the union of a man and a woman in marriage has been seen as the foundation on which a family is based. As such, Article 16 (1) of the UDHR upholds the right for two people to marry, stating that "Men and women of full age, without any limitations due to race, nationality, or religion, have the right to marry and to found a family."

"the foundation on which a family is based"

(Right) A four-year-old bride with her young husband in India after their arranged marriage.
(Below) Couples in arranged marriages do not always meet before the ceremony.

A suitable arrangement

In the western world people now usually choose their own marriage partners. This was not always so and most marriages used to be arranged. Arranged marriages still happen in some parts of the world or within certain religions and cultures. Many Indian families who have settled outside of India, such as Keiran's parents who left India in the 1960s, still uphold the tradition of arranged marriage. Often the most important aspect is the bond between the two families, rather than the relationship between the two people being married. Indeed, in some of the developing countries, small children can be pledged to marry in order to secure property or land or protect social status. In some Hindu families, the bride and groom often do not meet until the wedding ceremony. Keiran's parents married after only having seen a photograph of each other.

(Above) In the UK, as in many western countries, most people choose their own partners. Even though the individual concerned may think this is better than an arranged marriage, the divorce rate in some countries is so high that it is difficult to claim that one system is so much better than the other.

(Right) In traditional societies, the refusal of marriage or the wish to divorce are not always options that the poorer women of those societies can afford to take.

Different rules

As with arranged marriages, there are huge differences across the world's cultures in the rules about who can marry and when. In some cultures it is legal for a man to have more than one wife, or for children to be pledged to each other.

The Declaration of Human Rights upholds the importance of marriage being entered into with the "full and free consent" of both parties. Where the bride and groom have not met each other, or where children are pledged to one another, can each person really give their full consent, or agreement, to marry someone they do not know?

Supporters of the custom of arranged marriages say that divorce rates are lower than those among western society because

parents are older and wiser and so can choose more suitable partners for their children. The counter-argument is that the pressures of society as a whole and the two families concerned keep the marriage together whether it is a good relationship or not. In addition, for some women in very traditional environments, marriage can be their only option. Unlike Keiran, many are not given the education or opportunities to allow them to have careers and, therefore, economic independence. Faced with the possible prospect of extreme poverty, few women in these circumstances risk saying no to a marriage or seek a divorce if it is unsatisfactory.

Issue:
Equal rights
within a
marriage
Place:
Mali

Pene lives in Niaming near the River Niger in Mali. She is married to M'golo. Niele is also married to M'golo—she is his second wife. Pene and Niele have to work very hard, fetching water, gathering wood, planting crops, grinding rice, cooking, and caring for the collective children. Under Islamic law, M'golo can have four wives.

Pene would like to see M'golo marry again. If he were to take another wife, it would considerably ease both Pene's and Niele's workload. Pene says that men are not very good at anything except fishing!

An unequal partnership

The UDHR states that men and women are "entitled to equal rights as to marriage [or] during marriage." However, in many countries marriage customs clearly abuse the human rights issues that are supported by the Declaration. The Declaration acknowledges cultural differences in marriage, but says that human rights should not be denied. Throughout the world, for most of recorded history, marriage has often been a distinctly unequal partnership—regardless of the culture or country.

Women were commonly regarded as their husband's property, and traditionally their chief duty as a wife was to produce sons and heirs. If their husbands were rich, they lived in relative comfort with servants to do most of the hard work of looking after the children and running the household. Poor women had to look after their husbands, raise the children, and work the land or help in the family business. On marriage, anything that belonged to the woman often became her husband's property.

It is only relatively recently that women in the western world have been recognized in their own right—but their position in society has not always been acknowledged.

"her husband's property"

(Top and right) In countries like Mali, where women do most of the hard labor, the right of a man to have more than one wife is often seen as an advantage—it reduces the workload.

Date:
2001
Place:
Hereford,
England
The issue:
No marriage,
no pension

Anna Homsi, the pregnant 10-year partner of Brad Tinnion, a 28-year-old SAS soldier, was grief-stricken when he was killed in Sierra Leone in 2000 as SAS troops rescued six British soldiers held hostage. More sadness came the following year when the Ministry of Defence denied her a war pension.

Although Anna, 30, received a £20,000 ($37,000) once-only payment and an annual £2,000 grant until her daughter, Georgia, became 17, she did not qualify for an £18,000 annual pension because she was not married. Despite living together for a decade, Anna and Brad had not done so for six months before he joined the Army, which the pension regulations required.

Anna threatened to sue the Ministry of Defence. Because of her strong stance, the Ministry increased her once-only payment to £250,000 and in March 2003 announced that all unmarried partners of any British service personnel, even same-sex partners, will now receive pensions.

When is a couple not a couple? When they are not married and their relationship ends. Then, however long the relationship, they may find they have few legal rights.

Losing touch with their children is a fear faced by most parents when their partnership breaks down. Research has shown that children fear this, too.

"official stamp of marriage"

A nontraditional arrangement

As societies have changed, different types of family have evolved—traditional marriages do not always form the basis of family life. Many couples in western societies have decided that they do not want the official stamp of marriage. They have opted to cohabit—to live together without being officially married.

In Australia, prior to 1978, the legal rights of cohabitees were few. In 1978, however,

17

the Australian government recognized the need to protect the rights of cohabitees, acknowledging the status of such relationships. Cohabiting is recognized by the UDHR as forming a "common household" and the rights aimed at protecting people within marriage and family life are extended to people who choose not to marry but to live together. However, not all countries have made this progress. In the UK, even by 2004, co-habitees had few legal rights.

Date:
2004
Place:
San Francisco, California
Issue:
The right of anyone to marry

Although people in California voted in 2000 to define marriage as being between a man and woman, San Francisco officials decided gay couples had the same right to marry. Beginning on February 12, 2004, the city issued 4,161 marriage licenses to same-sex couples. Governor Arnold Schwarzenegger, however, ordered the attorney general to stop the weddings, and the California Supreme Court ended them on March 11. Local leaders in New Mexico, New Jersey, and New York also performed gay marriages. And the Massachusetts Supreme Court ruled they could begin on May 17, 2004. Some states responded by passing laws that only a man and woman could marry. Even President George W. Bush said he favored a ban on gay marriages.

Pictures of gay couples celebrating their marriages in San Francisco sent shock waves though the USA. Many of the couples came from other states and even foreign countries.

The gay pride movement in different countries has worked hard to improve the position of homosexual people, trying to ensure that they have the same rights as other members of society. However, they face strong opposition, particularly from those who regard homosexuality as a threat to family life.

A fair attitude?

Just as some people decide that they do not want the formal statement of marriage, other groups within society try to have their relationships officially recognized by the law of their country. Marriage can be seen as a statement of commitment. It is a public contract acknowledging the decision of two people to join their lives together. As such, it could be argued that established homosexual couples—couples of the same sex—who wish to show their pride in their relationship should be allowed to marry as well.

The question of gay and lesbian marriages is a controversial one, with feelings riding high on both sides of the argument. As society has evolved, the UN Commission has looked at the application of the Univeral Declaration of Human Rights in the light of changing social needs. It acknowledges that homosexuality between two consenting, or willing, adults is a matter for the individuals concerned. Some countries, however, have taken the first steps to extend the marriage rights in the UDHR for heterosexual (male and female) couples to homosexual couples. In 1989, Denmark became the first country officially to allow gay and lesbian weddings.

The first legally recognized homosexual wedding in Denmark took place in October 1989. Such an event illustrates that as society changes and different groups try to have their rights acknowledged, there are instances when governments will respond by changing the law of their country.

Rights for divorcees

Not all those who *are* able to marry, wish to stay that way. It is a sad fact that many people seek to end their marriages. Indeed, many believe that divorce is a human right, arguing that it is not good to force people to stay in an unhappy relationship. The UDHR states in Article 16 (1) that partners of a marriage should be treated equally "at its dissolution," acknowledging that in some instances the breakdown of a marriage is unavoidable. In early 2004 over one in two marriages in the US and one in three in Europe ended in divorce.

While the UDHR encourages governments to protect the rights of each person, the laws concerned with divorce vary from country to country. In the UK, provisions for supporting any children of the marriage are included in the divorce settlement, but the ex-wife's position can be less

"forced to stay together"

secure. Where both parents work, it is still more usual for the woman to give up her career to bring up the family. To break her ability to earn in this way affects the amount of pension a woman is able to claim when she retires.

Until 1996, a woman in the UK was not automatically allowed to have any of her husband's pension. Pressure groups worked to have the law changed. They successfully argued that pensions are to help retired people have a decent standard of living and to enable a wife, who has taken a career break to bring up the family, to have a secure future.

If a marriage turns sour, should a couple be forced to stay together? Wouldn't it be better for them, and their children, if they divorced? But then the daily arguments may be replaced by arguments over the children about when the absent parent can see them and for how long. And what about the pressures on the children who may feel loyalty to both parents? Can there ever be any winners?

In Sweden, women are able to put in a claim for access to their husband's pension in the event of a divorce. A similar right for women in the UK was only passed in 1996. The government recognized the plight of many women who found that because they had given up their careers to bring up children, they had little or no pension when they retired.

A different set of rules

As a contrast, the rights of married couples in Sweden are slightly different. In marriage, each partner has an "interest" in the other's property. If the couple divorce the estate is split in half, unless a written agreement was signed before the marriage declaring that certain belongings should remain in the possession of one person only. Where there are pensions, each person is entitled to put in a claim to have part access to their partner's income and it is up to the court to decide if and how the pensions should be divided.

"respect the rights of their partner"

To start a family is to take on new responsibilities—to one's partner as well as to the child. Successful families manage to adapt to these changes, although it may not always be easy.

Taking responsibility

It is important that individuals feel that their rights within marriage or partnerships are being upheld by the laws of the land—that they can enjoy an equal relationship. But it is also important that each individual should look on their role in the partnership with responsibility as well. Everyone has a responsibility to respect the rights of their partner: this may mean that they have to question some of the traditions or behavior that they have been brought up to believe is acceptable if it limits the rights of the other person. Responsibilities increase when a couple decide to start a family— and rights within the home need to reflect the changing needs that having a family brings.

Date:
1980–today
Place:
China
The issue:
Who decides a family's size?

China has the largest population in the world. In 2004 it stood at more than 1.3 billion. The population is so big that, inevitably, each year an enormous number of babies is born —more than the country can cope with. The Chinese government has been aware of this problem for some years. In 1980, to try to slow down the

(Right) The ideal family, Chinese style— a smiling couple with their son.
(Below) China's huge population is why only one child per family is allowed.

growth in the population, it introduced a policy of limiting each Chinese couple to a family of just one child.

Chinese culture has a long tradition of favoring boys. With only one legal chance to have a son, many families resort to desperate measures to make sure that their child is the "right" sex. It is estimated that since 1979 up to 50 million girl babies have simply "disappeared."

Thousands of unwanted baby girls end up in China's state-run orphanages. In 1991, China signed the International Convention on the Rights of the Child, committing itself to protect children's rights. In spite of this, a group called Human Rights Watch found that many of these unwanted babies and children were neglected and left to die in the orphanages. It is not only children who are suffering—there have also been reports of women heavily pregnant with a second child being forced to have an abortion.

A meeting of the Chinese Communist Party in Beijing. The rapidly increasing population is a huge problem, overstretching resources, resulting in direct action from the state.

State interference?

Is the Chinese government right to restrict the number of children in a family? This policy seems to disregard Article 16 of the UDHR. Clause 1 of the article states that "Men and women of full age…have the right to marry and found a family." Clause 3 of the same article says: "The family is the natural and fundamental group unit of society and is entitled to protection by society and the State."

A difficulty with the UDHR is how it is interpreted. For thousands of years, China has been ruled by authoritarian governments, and today's Communist government is just one more in that long line. All of these governments have regarded the good of the whole state as far more important than the rights of individuals.

Today, the Chinese government could quite reasonably argue that they are supporting Article 16. They are not stopping couples from having a family, and by limiting the size of each family they are trying to make sure that there will be enough resources to provide for and protect each family, so ensuring the good of everyone.

But what of ordinary Chinese people? Article 12 of the UDHR reads: "No one shall be subjected to arbitrary interference with his privacy, family [or] home…" It could be argued that China's one-child policy subjects its citizens to "arbitrary [unnecessary] interference" by dictating the size of the family by law—and enforcing the law with tough penalties, such as forcible abortion.

(Top left) Fetuses in jars are displayed at a birth-control exhibition in China. People are told that having more than one child may mean that later ones are deformed. This message is reinforced by family planning posters showing happy parents and their only child.

Another "solution" to a growing population

China is not the only country where governments have attempted to limit the size of families. India's population is also increasing at a rate that the government fears will swamp its resources. In the late 1980s, in an attempt to deal with this problem, the government of Mrs. Indira Gandhi (left) introduced a program to provide men with free vasectomies, an operation that prevents them from making a woman pregnant. It was not successful. Much of the program was carried out in rural areas where large families are seen as the only way of providing security for the parents' old age—there are no state pensions so elderly parents rely on the support of their children. Those who carried out the program were educated people from towns and cities. As such they were regarded with fear and suspicion by the local people who saw them as the traditional oppressors of rural communities. The government stopped the

"oppressors of the rural communities"

program, admitting that it had been heavy-handed. Even though education programs on contraception for women are used instead, the population keeps on growing—at a rate of approximately 15 million a year. That's nearly three times the population of Massachusetts!

(Left) A health worker explains contraception to a countrywoman.

Are there any answers?

Family size tends to drop as family wealth and education increases. All over the world, as people are more able to provide for themselves by getting good jobs and they become wealthier, birth rates fall. In the USA, for example, the average number of children born to a woman in 1800 was seven. In 2004 it was two. This is a big drop, but it has taken nearly two centuries to achieve.

The real problem is time. Even if countries like India and China could provide the education and jobs that help lead to greater prosperity and falling populations, is there time? The world population by mid-2003 was 6.3 billion. It is estimated that it will double by 2050.

A family belonging to the Laestadius church in Finland. Members of this religion do not believe in contraception, so many families within this religion are large. This couple have twenty children, the mother has been pregnant for a total of fifteen years.

Date: 2004
Place: Finland
The issue: Do individual couples have the right to an unlimited number of children?

Like most developed countries, the birthrate in Finland is quite low: 1.7 children per couple. However, members of the Finnish Laestadius church often have as many as twenty children. They say that their religion bans contraception. Like the other Scandinavian countries, Finland has a very generous system of state benefits. It pays $330 per month for the first child and $100 for the second, with poor mothers receiving an extra $200 per month.

The people of the Laestadius church are being allowed to act in accordance with their beliefs—another right upheld by the UDHR (Article 18). The Finnish government has upheld the right of members of its country to go about their family life in privacy and without unnecessary interference, in accordance with Article 12. But many Finnish taxpayers resent having to subsidize such huge families. They also believe that with the world's rapidly increasing population, having such large families is highly irresponsible.

Education may help to improve living standards and reduce population growth, but it is an expensive and slow process.

And if you can't have a family?

Article 16 of the Universal Declaration of Human Rights supports the right of men and women to have a family. Even just 30 years ago if a couple could not have a family they probably felt sad, but accepted that was that, there was nothing anyone could do about it.

But today, thanks to advances in medical science, it *is* possible to do something about it. Fertility treatments, such as drugs to encourage women to ovulate and IVF (in-vitro fertilization, where the ovum, or egg, is fertilized by a sperm outside the womb), are now common. In fact they are so common that even couples who once would not

have been able to start a family have entered the category of those with "rights" to have one. However, such treatments are expensive. Should the right to have a child be available to any woman, or only to those who can afford it? And should "any" woman mean exactly that, or should it be restricted to those who are in a stable relationship, or to those who are employed? What about people who are disabled, either physically or mentally?

"Should the 'right' to have a child be available to any woman?"

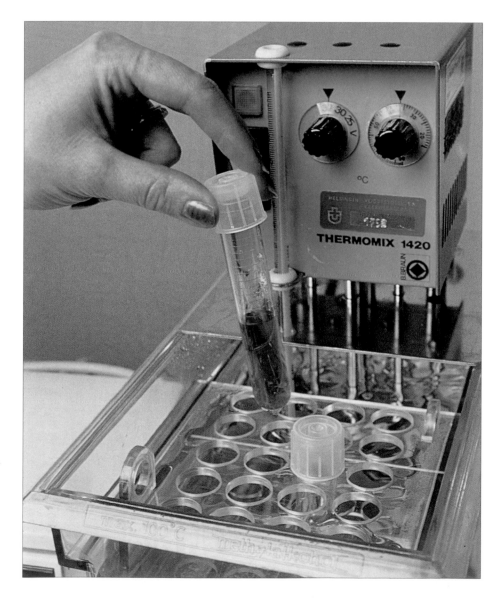

As advances are made in medical science the ethical issues that face society, and that need to be addressed by organizations and governments, become more and more complex. However, one issue that will remain constant, whatever the medical changes, is that whoever has the right to have a child has a responsibility to that child.

At a clinic treating infertility in Helsinki, Finland, sperm and eggs are put into test tubes in the hope that fertilization, which has not occurred in the mother's body, will take place successfully out of it.

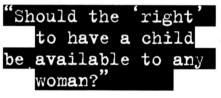

Date:
1919
Place:
London
The issue:
Rights for children "beyond any consideration of race, nationality, or creed"

In 1919, Eglantyne Jebb founded Save the Children, which has become one of the world's leading voluntary aid organizations. She was born in 1876 into a family of prosperous landowners. After studying at Oxford she joined the Charity Organization Society and in 1906 wrote *Cambridge: A study in social questions*. It was a pioneering work and made her aware of poverty, bad housing, and other social issues. This was followed by work for various charities in Europe. The horrors she saw there during the First World War prompted her, and her sister Dorothy, to set up The Save the Children Fund, to aid children "beyond any consideration of race, nationality, or creed." She organized campaigns to bring the plight of certain groups of children to the attention of the world, raising £400,000—the equivalent of $15 million today.

Eglantyne Jebb (1876–1928) founded Save the Children and pioneered the idea of children's rights. Her work formed the basis of the UN's Declaration of the Rights of the Child.

In 1923, Miss Jebb made perhaps an even greater contribution to the well-being of children: a declaration of their rights. This was adopted by the League of Nations the following year and formed the basis of the UN Declaration of the Rights of the Child in 1959 and the International Convention on the Rights of the Child in 1989. Miss Jebb also began exploring ways to extend the Fund's work to Africa and Asia—urging people to work with a country's culture, instead of trying to make them adopt western methods.

By the end of the 19th century children no longer worked in mines, but many still worked in appalling conditions. Miss Jebb helped to improve their lives.

A new approach

Miss Jebb believed that all children had rights as individuals: they were entitled to just as much consideration and respect as adults—a very unusual attitude to children at that time. From the start, Save the Children had no religious or political basis because, as its founder put it, "The only international language is a child's cry."

Few people before Eglantyne Jebb had recognized children's rights in this way. Earlier social reformers had protested about children being employed in bad conditions: down the mines, in factories, and sweeping chimneys. Others had tried to ensure that even the very poorest had some education. Although there was no free health service in the 19th century anywhere in the world, many doctors did not charge poor families for their services. But these measures were generally on a small scale. And at this time most children were seen as "belonging" to their parents—rather as married women "belonged" to their husbands.

The rights of children

Eglantyne Jebb's work was very important in getting countries and governments to recognize the rights of children. The 1989 International Convention on the Rights of the Child was signed by 180 nations from around the world. It brought the issue of children's rights into international law.

While fundamental rights such as health, protection, and living standards are all addressed by the International Convention on the Rights of the Child, the document also highlights the importance of providing children with a good education. The right to play and recreation is included as a right as it is seen as an important part of childhood.

A child in New York is vaccinated against flu. Today it is easy to take for granted the view that everyone, child or adult, has the same rights.

Many children in developing countries work long hours in poor conditions for little pay, just as children in Europe and North America did in the last century.

Different societies, different rights

Inevitably, as in every other field of human rights, different cultures see "rights" in different ways. For children in developed countries the "right" to leisure time does not seem out of place. But in the developing nations where there is great poverty and the annual income of most adults is much less than $200, everyone in the family is struggling to survive. Can a child's right to play be seen as realistic then?

(Right) For all too many children playing is a luxury. Time and again, aid workers report that in places where there is civil war, social upheaval, famine, or great poverty, the children do not know, or have forgotten, how to play.

Date: Today
Place: Philippines and Thailand
Issue: The exploitation of children

In Southeast Asia children, mostly girls, are exploited for sex. Tourists from developed countries visit countries, such as Thailand and the Philippines, just for sex. This "sex tourism" is not new, but the spread of AIDS means that fear of infection has caused many of the "tourists" to turn from women to girls as young as ten, believing (often wrongly) that such children cannot have had sex very often and so cannot be infected.

Protecting the vulnerable

Children, being young and vulnerable, are open to exploitation, especially if their families are very poor. Pedophilia (sexual acts with children) is illegal. Such abuse happens in many countries behind closed doors. In poorer countries, such as the Philippines or Thailand where some families are desperate for any income, they do not always question how money is earned. The pathetic sums they are given for their children does, briefly, make life easier. This, of course, makes stopping child prostitution and protecting children from sexual abuse even more difficult.

The press and media are often criticized for intruding, but they have played an important role in making people and governments aware of such abuses. And governments in Europe, Southeast Asia, and the USA, are taking steps to tackle the problems of sex tourists. In September 2003, President George W. Bush signed the Protect Act making it illegal for U.S. citizens to travel abroad and engage in sex with a minor.

But abuse of children is not confined to Third World and developing countries.

abuse of children

The issue:
What is a good parent and can a child decide?

Place:
Florida

Gregory Kingsley's mother—were her rights ignored when he "divorced" her?

Twelve-year-old Gregory Kingsley was put into care by his mother because she felt unable to look after him when she separated from his father. Gregory went to live with a foster family. He got on so well with them that his mother, Rachel Kingsley, became worried and wanted him back. Gregory did not want to go back to her. To make sure he didn't, he hired a lawyer and went to court to have his mother's legal rights withdrawn.

After Gregory won his case many people were worried that the real reason he wanted to stay with his foster parents was that they were much richer than his mother.

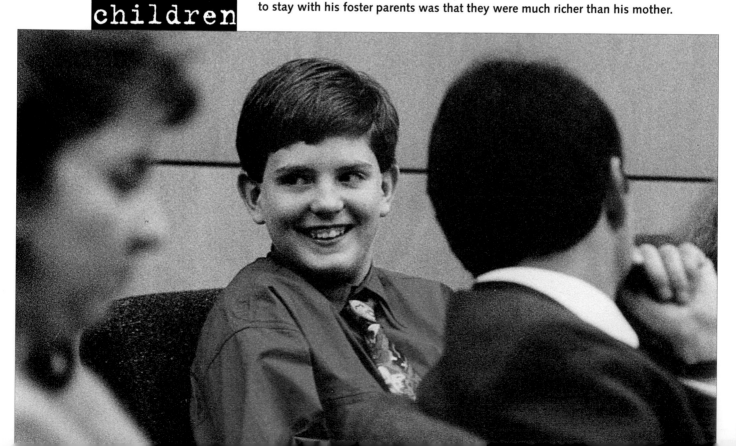

The International Convention on the Rights of the Child lays down standards that the nations who have agreed to be bound by it try to follow. But trying to address society's problems is expensive, and some countries find it harder to provide basic rights for their citizens than others.

"state court proceedings"

Eglantyne Jebb felt strongly that relief could be brought to children throughout the world. Education programs in many countries, such as Peru, have been set up by Save the Children.

Making legal history

Gregory made legal history. He was the first child in the USA to go to court to assert his rights against a parent. It was claimed that his mother had abused him, leaving him alone for long periods and not caring for him properly.

One of the main messages of the International Convention on the Rights of the Child was that whenever an official decision was made that affected the child, the child's interests should be seen as significant. While the interests of the parents or the state are considered, they should not be seen as all-important.

The International Convention supports this view, but it is up to each country to enforce it through law. And even though Gregory Kingsley won his case, the USA did not actually have an overall children's policy. The U.S. government did not sign the International Convention on the Rights of the Child until 1995, and in 2004 it remained the only nation that had not formally approved it.

Date: 2002
Place: UK
The issue: Domestic violence and self-protection

Donna Tinker, a 32-year-old mother of three, lived with her abusive husband, Richard, in Harrogate, North Yorkshire. He was very jealous and often hit her. After one argument on June 13, 1999, he kicked her in the face, giving her a broken tooth, bruised jaw, and black eye. Later in the kitchen he held his arm around her neck and threatened to press a hot iron against her face. Donna panicked and grabbed the nearest thing she could reach, a small knife. She struck out and punctured her husband's lung. He died a week later.

"Donna panicked and grabbed the nearest thing she could"

During the trial, no witnesses were called for Donna's defense. The jury was told that the iron was found in the kitchen cupboard. Her defense of provocation was not accepted, and they found her guilty in April 2000. Donna was sentenced to life imprisonment. During her appeal, however, a statement was finally introduced that neighbors had given to police on the day of the stabbing. It said they had found the iron on the floor and put it into the cupboard. On December 5, 2002, three judges quashed the murder conviction and substituted manslaughter, setting Donna's sentence at seven years. She was released in December 2003.

Many women suffer from domestic abuse at the hands of their violent partners. In some extreme cases they are forced to defend themselves. Emma Humphries (shown left) was also wrongly convicted of murdering her partner.

Safety in the home?

Cases such as Donna Tinker's and Emma Humphries' made the legal profession in the UK look again at how the law dealt with domestic violence—physical, sexual, and mental abuse of a person by their partner.

Many of the articles in the UDHR uphold the importance of personal safety (Article 3) and the right of each individual to equality. Article 16 specifically refers to the importance of equal rights in marriage. International statistics show, however, that in the very place you would hope to feel safe, within your family environment or your home, many women from different backgrounds, across different cultures and races, suffer abuse at the hands of their partners.

Amnesty International launched a global campaign in March 2004 to cut violence against women, saying one in three women suffer serious violence worldwide. Statistics from the FBI in 2002 recorded 57,000 individuals killed in the USA in incidents of family violence over the previous 25 years. The U.S. Bureau of Justice documents nearly 700,000 incidents of domestic violence each year.

Emergency services in the UK receive one call every minute about family violence. In Australia, Victoria police alone received 21,622 reports of family violence in 2000-2001, with 77% of the victims being women. In Pakistan, there are an estimated 1,000 "honor killings" of women each year.

Zero Tolerance

As a result of the Emma Humphries trial and subsequent cases in the UK, the issue of domestic violence has been brought much more to the attention of the public and government. In Scotland, in 1992, the Zero Tolerance

(Left) Justice is supposed to be quite fair, so the figure of Justice wears a blindfold, to show she cannot be influenced.

(Above) Calls to special children's helplines suggest child abuse is probably more common than most people realize.

Campaign was launched to generate debate about the concern for the lack of protection for women. It was so successful that it was adopted by other countries around the world, and their governments were also lobbied to uphold women's rights in their homes.

It is not just women who suffer domestic violence. Some men also suffer at the hands of their female partners, although the statistics indicate that there are fewer such incidents. But there is a stigma attached to being mistreated for both men and women, and many instances go unreported.

Vulnerable children

Children are also vulnerable. If they are abused it is far more difficult for them to escape. For years an adult's word was believed rather than a child's. As with domestic violence, abusers of children come from all different backgrounds, races, and nationalities. Now, helplines set up especially for children receive huge numbers of calls from children of different ages who are abused at home. And there is much greater awareness of the dangers children face.

Date: 2002
Issue: Are all carers caring?
Place: Illinois

Violette King could see that her father was in distress when she visited him at a nursing home in an Illinois suburb of St. Louis, Missouri. Louis Papagianis, 85, had scratches, bruises, and cuts on his neck, arms, cheek, and behind his ears. He had been abused by a nurse's aide who was reported by other nurses's aides to the home's administrator. "My father had become combative," said Mrs. King. "Now I understand why. He was trying to save his own life." When nothing was done for eight months, she filed a complaint. After a hearing, the abuser lost her right to work in nursing homes in that state.

This case was one of many that the General Accounting Office, an investigative arm of Congress, presented to the U.S. Senate Special Committee on Aging in 2002. They told of physical and sexual abuse of nursing home residents, cases that were not reported promptly to local authorites and rarely prosecuted. Some 1.6 million Americans live in about 17,000 nursing homes, and more than one-third of those homes have been cited by state inspectors for violations that harmed residents or placed them in immediate jeopardy.

Many of the homes for elderly people provide a good standard of care and a sense of community for those who live there, but sadly there are a few exceptions.

Prevention and protection

At the other end of the age range to children, elderly people are also at risk. Elder abuse, the lack of appropriate action or care for an elderly person by other members of their family or a carer, is now recognized as a real problem. Abuse can take many forms. It can be physical or sexual. There can also be psychological abuse, when the elderly person may be shouted at, embarrassed, or intimidated. Financial abuse happens when relatives or the carer take money or property without permission. Neglect is when everyday, basic help is not supplied.

"protection is available through the courts"

There are two ways that governments can work to uphold elderly people's rights to be treated properly. These are through laws to prevent abuse or to protect people from abuse.

Protection is available through the courts. Countries including

Elder abuse doesn't only happen within families. Even in special accommodation, elderly people may not be treated with the dignity that is their right.

Canada, the USA, and Australia have specific legislation to protect elderly people. Though most Europeans countries do not have such laws, there is general legislation that can be applied, such as public health acts.

There are many organizations that work to promote the rights of elderly people through raising awareness about the problems, promoting research, and providing information to educate the public and governments. One such organization in the UK with European links, Action on Elder Abuse, works to uphold the right of old people to be treated fairly, equally, and with dignity.

It is important to try to see people as individuals and not "issues" so that they may be treated with dignity.

The Mexican government spends large sums of money promoting its image as a modern society in an effort to win respect from the governments of developed countries. Mexico joined the North American Free Trade Agreement with Canada and the USA and wants to be taken seriously as a modern 21st-century nation.

(Above) This is how tourists see Mexico, but for a very large number of Mexicans the view is rather different (right).

Date: 2004
Place: Mexico
The issues: The right to an acceptable standard of living

Tourists flock to the resorts of Mexico's Pacific coast, to enjoy a good time in the bars and clubs of places like Acapulco. Travel less than 125 miles from the beaches and you enter a different world. A world where the shacks of the local people have earthen floors and no running water, electricity, or sanitation. Children go barefoot and their fathers earn about $1.50 a day tending crops of coffee and corn on land belonging to powerful landowners.

On the other hand it uses distinctly old-fashioned ways of dealing with anyone who wants to make the distribution of wealth in the country a little less unequal. When Mexican citizens have demonstrated to demand essential materials that are needed in order for them to do their jobs properly and earn a better living, they have often been brutally treated. There are instances when people have been killed.

A blind eye to justice

Article 25 (1) of the UDHR reads: "Everyone has the right to a standard of living adequate for the health and well-being of himself and of his family, including food, clothing, housing and medical care, and necessary social services, and the right to security in the event of unemployment, sickness, disability, widowhood, old age, or other lack of livelihood in circumstances beyond his control.'

"help people to help themselves"

While the aims of the UDHR are common to all countries, the differences in the culture and wealth of each country affects how far the goals of the UDHR can be achieved. However, at the very least, basic human rights should be met— such as people's needs for food and water, shelter, clothing, sanitation, health services, and education.

Additionally, the UDHR encourages all governments to help people to help themselves to achieve these basic standards through being able to work. But it is sometimes easier for governments to put down demonstrations than to address far-reaching human rights problems. These might threaten their position of power or could be both costly and time-consuming to try to deal with.

And baby goes too, strapped to his mother's back. Many Mexican people struggle to achieve a basic standard of living, so every member of a family who can work does. For women, there is no such thing as maternity leave or welfare.

The issue:
The right to dignity
Place: Paris

A healthy lifestyle

Good living conditions are crucial in order to ensure that people remain healthy and well. When their health is already poor and their living conditions below standard, people are more susceptible to diseases such as tuberculosis, a wasting disease that affects the lungs in particular, dysentery, and cholera.

Therefore, hostels like Chapsa are, important in tackling these health issues—providing homeless people with facilities to wash and change, eat, and receive vital medical care. But there is another consideration.

Each night in Paris the police pick up some of the city's 15,000 homeless people and take them to the Centre d'Hebergement et d'Assistance aux Personnes Sans Abri (Chapsa). This is a former beggars' prison which takes in up to 250 people a day.

Tonight these two will have a bed instead of a sidewalk. The treatment of people in some hostels is so harsh, however, that they may wonder if it is worth it.

In some countries, the state or private businesses invest in special, low-rent accommodations, specifically to help people in need.

"the end of the civilized world"

At Chapsa, the homeless people are fed and washed, reclothed, and given medical treatment; but they are handled in a way that is often rough and humiliating. The showers are filthy and the bunk beds crowded, with rubber mattresses and no sheets to sleep on. According to a photographer who went on one of the nightly roundups, the atmosphere of the old jail hung heavily over everything: "It was the end of the civilized world, a completely hostile, violent, hopeless environment."

The UDHR also asserts that people are "equal in dignity and rights." Is it acceptable, then, that homeless people should be treated so harshly? Is it possible to provide the same services and aid in a way that could help them to take pride in themselves?

Self-help, not charity is the idea behind *The Big Issue.* It gives the people who sell it the chance to get back on their feet, regain their self-respect, and, with luck, rebuild their lives.

Self-help

The recession (a decline in a country's wealth) in industry in the developed world throughout the late 1980s and early 1990s caused huge job losses. The cutbacks meant that each year there were thousands fewer jobs for high school graduates, far fewer in fact than there were people to apply for them. The result of this soon became visible on city streets: more and more people, especially young people like Mark, homeless and begging.

Without a home, it is all the more difficult to find work. But if you are so poor that you have to beg, however can you afford a home? This, to the founders of a specialist magazine, was the "big issue." And that is what the first UK magazine to help the homeless was called. An extension of the idea behind the street newspapers of the USA, it is sold on town and city streets only by homeless people or people who are still struggling to get back on their feet. Out in all weathers, it is not a particularly easy way to earn money, but it is a start. Perhaps even more importantly, homeless people are being given the power to help themselves. The project has been so successful it is now being copied elsewhere in Europe as well as in South Africa.

If you do not have a home you have few rights. Without an address the authorities cannot contact you, so you don't exist. If you don't exist you cannot claim any welfare you may be entitled to.

**Place: London
The issue: An alternative to begging**

Mark had a successful job in real estate. He earned a good salary and could afford to live comfortably. But Mark was laid off and then lost his job. Unable to pay his rent and unwilling to return to his family where he had experienced difficulties in the past, he found himself sleeping on the streets.

Mark then got in touch with the magazine for homeless people, *The Big Issue,* and became a vendor, selling copies of the magazine. Through this, he gradually saved enough money for a deposit on renting a new apartment—the next step in getting his life back to where it was before.

HOME AS A SANCTUARY

Date: November 9, 1938
Place: Germany
Issue: A complete loss of human rights

After a night of anti-Jewish rioting, storekeepers face the wreckage of their shops in Berlin in November 1938. This was one of many extreme abuses of human rights that the Nazis in Germany would carry out against the Jews and other minority groups until their defeat and Hitler's suicide in 1945.

On the night of November 9, 1938, Jewish communities across Germany were subjected to the most horrific campaign of terror. Jewish homes and property were broken into, businesses were raided, windows were smashed, and belongings looted. More terrifyingly, Jewish people were beaten up in the streets by rampaging Nazi Stormtroopers and German civilians alike. Jews were beaten unconscious with lead piping while crowds of people looked on. The event became known as *Kristallnacht* ("night of broken glass").

The number of deaths among the Jewish community was never given—but there was no doubt that thousands of Jewish people were terrorized and killed, with thousands more being evicted from their homes in subsequent raids throughout Germany.

Annoyed by the cost of clearing up the damage, a senior Nazi Party member, Hermann Goering, is said to have remarked that they "should have killed more Jews and broken less glass."

No laws—no protection

As the leader of the Nazi party, Adolf Hitler increased his own power. With this power, he took away the basic rights of others, particularly the European Jews. He blamed them and other minority groups for the economic difficulties that Germany was experiencing at the time. He took away their rights first in Germany and then, after the outbreak of the Second World War, in every country the Germans occupied. He took their possessions, drove them from their homes, and finally took the lives of 11 million people from minority groups.

Synagogues, too, were destroyed in the *Kristallnacht* destruction.

The world saw the most complete disregard for people's rights to live in peace and safety. The state, which should have protected them, persecuted them. There were no laws to help them because the laws themselves had been changed.

Article 12 of the UDHR—stating that no one should ever be subjected to unnecessary interference within the privacy of their home and family—responds directly to events under the Nazi regime. Article 17 states clearly that everyone is entitled to own their own property, which should not be taken away without good reason.

It was hoped that the UDHR and the pressure of each country upon every other would prevent such fundamental attacks on human rights from ever happening again.

"*fundamental attacks on human rights*"

Human suffering and the violation of human rights are still part of our lives today. This is why the UDHR is still such an important document and each government and nation should want to achieve the standard it sets.

The role of government

While the UN makes its goals quite clear through the UDHR, the Declaration is not legally binding. It is up to each country's government to pass laws to uphold the rights of their citizens. And where laws do exist, these need upholding. Despite the lessons learned through history, there are still instances today of large-scale disregard for human rights. Civil wars in the former Yugoslavia and Rwanda have resulted in millions of refugees and prisoners of war who live in fear for their lives.

However, even when governments strive to do their best by their citizens, it can be a matter of opinion between what is seen as offering protection and what may be interpreted as state interference.

The right to privacy in one's own home

Place:
Montana

The USA is a huge country and many parts are sparsely inhabited. In some remote neighborhoods the authorities do not always know what people are up to. In the state of Montana there are a number of communities of self-styled "mountain men." These men reject all government authority; they refuse to pay their taxes or license their vehicles. Many hold extreme views, being violently against rights for gay people or people from ethnic minorities. Many of the Montana "mountain men" have been found to be well supplied with guns and ammunition, the right of every American citizen to bear arms being something they do support. Members of one such community were arrested for blowing up the state government building in Oklahoma City in 1995.

As a result of such acts of terrorism, the authorities now take a much closer interest in these groups. This serves to make them feel their concerns about interference are justified.

An attempt by the U.S. authorities to discover what was going on in one community led to a shoot-out and the deaths of several people (on both sides of the law).

Behind closed doors

How far should the right to privacy in your own home go? Surely the right to be protected from "arbitrary interference" means that the government or police should not be allowed to invade your home without good reason? But what if, behind closed doors, you are using your privacy to make bombs that will take away the human rights of others? Should your right to privacy remain then?

A thin line

Clearly, there are instances when the state does need to intervene, in the interest of safety. But there is sometimes a fine line between a government acting

(Opposite) A stretcher is carried away from Pantglas Junior School, Aberfan, in Wales in the UK. On October 21, 1966, a pile of coal waste collapsed, burying the school and surrounding area, killing 144 people. The terrible disaster was reported as "news" by the media. But is it right that the grieving families should not be allowed to mourn in private (above)?

Feeling safe and happy is an important part of growing up. Perhaps if we all tried to take on the responsibilities of our position in the family, as parent, grandparent, brother, or sister, this would help to develop a sense of security within the home.

responsibly or actually taking away people's rights. There are occasions when the rights of one person will clash with another. The state must steer a careful path between the two. What happens, for instance, when a court must decide on a parent's access to see his or her child, while the other parent believes the child's safety is in danger? A right decision will ensure the child's protection, a wrong one will deny one parent his or her rights. Or should our rights to freedom of speech allow the media the freedom to intrude in the private lives of people?

Rights and responsibilities

It is not solely the responsibility of governments to protect human rights. It is a responsibility that we all share. We all want to have our own needs met and rights fulfilled, but rights always come with responsibilities.

Our homes should be places where we are able to feel safe—our families a source of support and security. The make-up of the family unit may vary throughout the world, and may have changed over time, but its role can be said to have remained much the same. If each person made the effort to look after the rights of others in the "small places, close to home" it would allow each one of us to develop within a safer environment.

Alongside this, it is up to the governments of each country to try to achieve laws that uphold the rights set out by the Universal Declaration of Human Rights to enable each of us to live safely within our homes and families.

Glossary

abortion: an operation that takes place in the early stages of pregnancy. The embryo, or unborn baby, is taken out of the mother's womb, preventing the pregnancy from continuing.

AIDS: Acquired Immune Deficiency Syndrome, an often fatal condition caused by a virus in the blood that attacks the body's immune system, so weakening its ability to defend the body against harmful organisms.

arbitrarily: something, such as a decision or course of action, that is taken at random and without warning. When something is done arbitrarily, it is rarely based on an informed or rational opinion.

authoritarian: a regime that requires unquestioning obedience to it rules and acceptance of its demands. Individual human rights are ignored by such regimes.

Communist: a member of the Communist party, a political organization based on the ideas put forward by Karl Marx and Friedrich Engels in the Communist Manifesto published in 1848. Based on the idea of communal (that is, state) ownership of the means of production (such as factories and farmland), it was intended that everyone should receive what they needed from the state in return for working for it according to their ability (doing what they did best, whether as a professional or manual worker).

consent: to agree to do something or to allow someone else to do something. For example, parents can give their consent to their child's marriage.

constitution: a collection of basic principles or an established set of rules, often used in terms of people's rights.

contraception: a means of deliberately preventing pregnancy. The most usual means of contraception in the developed world are the Pill and the cap for women and condoms for men.

creed: set of beliefs or religion.

culture: the shared beliefs and way of life of a particular group of people.

dissolution: bringing something to an end. This can be permanent, such as the ending of a marriage, or more temporary, when a parliament is dissolved before a general election to elect a new one.

domestic abuse/violence: physical, sexual, or mental abuse within the home of members of the family by other members within the family.

dowry: the property or money brought by a bride to her husband. Once common throughout the world, the custom is now largely restricted to developing countries, particularly India. Although the government there has banned the practice, it is so deeply rooted in tradition that a bride is still expected to provide a dowry.

economic issues: issues (or matters) that affect the economy (wealth) of a country or individual. Today, economic issues usually involve the financial (money) matters of a government, business or family.

ethical: when something is morally correct or honorable.

exploitation: taking advantage of someone or something. Exploitation of a natural resource such as oil means developing and making use of it. Exploitation of a person means taking advantage (making use) of someone, not for their good, but for the good of the person who is doing the exploiting. Throughout history, weaker members of society have been exploited by those who are more powerful, richer, or better educated. That is why the United Nations' UDHR and Convention on the Rights of the Child are so important. They will not stop human beings from exploiting each other, but they are acknowledgments that it is wrong to do so.

fundamental: absolutely basic.

heterosexual: someone who is sexually attracted to people of the opposite sex.

homosexual: someone who is sexually attracted to people of the same sex.

justice: fair treatment or outcome of court proceedings.

Laid off: losing a job through no fault of the worker. When workers are dismissed because they are no longer needed by the company for which they worked, they have been laid off.

League of Nations: an association of countries and states formed in 1919 to encourage international cooperation and peace. It was replaced by the United Nations in 1945.

nationality: belonging to a particular nation or country. Traditionally, all members of a nation were linked by a common language, religion, culture, and the fact that they lived in the

same part of the world. Today, emigration caused by wars and the movement of people to "new" countries, such as the USA, Canada, and New Zealand, has made "nationality" a much looser, less easily defined term, generally based on the country in which a person is born.

ovulate: in the female reproductive cycle, when an egg is released from the ovary.

ovum: the egg-cell produced by the female.

pension: a regular payment made by a government or employer to someone over retirement age or to widows or widowers. The payments are taken out of money that has been paid into a special fund by the individual, or by his or her spouse, during their working life in order to provide an income in their old age.

persecution: repeatedly attacking or treating someone badly.

sanctuary: a place of refuge.

spouse: a husband or wife.

terrorism: the use of violent, intimidating actions to try to force a government or community to take a particular action or follow a certain policy. It is bullying on a large scale.

tribunal: a group of people (often lawyers) appointed by a government to investigate a matter of public concern.

tuberculosis (TB): an infectious disease that affects the lungs. It is most common among very poor communities where the standard of living is low.

vasectomy: a minor procedure to adjust part of a man's testicles so that he will be unable to make a woman pregnant.

vicious circle: when one negative event leads onto another, making it almost impossible for someone caught up in the situations to break free. They may think things will never go right for them.

wedlock: a now rather old-fashioned term for marriage.

welfare: financial (monetary) provision provided by the state (government) to help support people who are unable to support themselves and their families properly.

widowhood: the state of being a widow. A married woman whose husband is dead is a widow. A man whose wife is dead is known as a widower.

Useful addresses

American Civil Liberties Union
125 Broad Street,
New York, NY 10004
www.aclu.org

Amnesty International USA
322 8th Ave.
New York, NY 10001
www.amnesty.org

Applied Research Center
3781 Broadway
Oakland, CA 94611
www.arc.org

Canadian Civil Liberties
Association
Suite 200, 394 Bloor Street West
Toronto, ON M5S 1X4
www.ccla.org

Center for Human Rights
Education
P.O. Box 311020
Atlanta, GA 31311
www.accessatlanta.com/communi
ty/groups/chre/

The Council of Canadians
502-151 Slater St.
Ottawa, Ontario, K1P 5H3
Canada
www.canadians.org

National Conference for
Community and Justice
71 5th Avenue, Suite 1100
New York, NY 10003
www.nccj.org

National Urban League, Inc.
120 Wall Street
New York, NY 10015
www.nul.org

Women Express
515 Washington Street, 6th Floor
Boston, MA 02111
www.teenvoices.com